EMMANUEL JOSEPH

The Cultural Compass, Navigating Entrepreneurship Through Psychology, Ethics, and Social Insight

Copyright © 2025 by Emmanuel Joseph

All rights reserved. No part of this publication may be reproduced, stored or transmitted in any form or by any means, electronic, mechanical, photocopying, recording, scanning, or otherwise without written permission from the publisher. It is illegal to copy this book, post it to a website, or distribute it by any other means without permission.

First edition

This book was professionally typeset on Reedsy.
Find out more at reedsy.com

Contents

1	Chapter 1: The Psychology of Entrepreneurship	1
2	Chapter 2: The Ethical Foundation of Entrepreneurship	3
3	Chapter 3: Social Insight and Market Understanding	5
4	Chapter 4: The Role of Innovation in Entrepreneurship	7
5	Chapter 5: The Entrepreneurial Ecosystem	9
6	Chapter 6: Building a Strong Brand	11
7	Chapter 7: Customer-Centric Entrepreneurship	12
8	Chapter 8: Leadership in Entrepreneurship	14
9	Chapter 9: Strategic Planning and Execution	16
10	Chapter 10: Financial Management and Sustainability	18
11	Chapter 11: Marketing and Customer Acquisition	20
12	Chapter 12: Operations and Supply Chain Management	22
13	Chapter 13: Risk Management and Crisis Response	24
14	Chapter 14: Scaling and Growth Strategies	26
15	Chapter 15: International Entrepreneurship	28
16	Chapter 16: Technology and Digital Transformation	30
17	Chapter 17: The Future of Entrepreneurship	32
18	Chapter 18: Continuous Improvement and Innovation	34
19	Chapter 19: Building a Resilient Organization	36
20	Chapter 20: The Future of Work and Entrepreneurship	38

1

Chapter 1: The Psychology of Entrepreneurship

Every successful entrepreneur possesses a unique set of psychological traits that enable them to navigate the turbulent waters of business. This chapter delves into the mind of an entrepreneur, exploring the critical attributes such as resilience, risk tolerance, and creativity. By understanding these traits, aspiring entrepreneurs can better prepare themselves for the challenges ahead and develop strategies to enhance their psychological resilience.

Moreover, the chapter examines the role of self-efficacy in entrepreneurial success. Self-efficacy, or the belief in one's ability to succeed, is a crucial determinant of entrepreneurial behavior. High self-efficacy can lead to greater persistence in the face of obstacles and a higher likelihood of achieving goals. By fostering a strong sense of self-efficacy, entrepreneurs can increase their chances of success.

The chapter also discusses the impact of cognitive biases on decision-making. Entrepreneurs often face high levels of uncertainty and must make decisions with incomplete information. Cognitive biases, such as overconfidence and the availability heuristic, can influence these decisions and lead to suboptimal outcomes. By recognizing and mitigating the effects of these biases, entrepreneurs can make more informed and rational decisions.

Finally, the chapter explores the importance of emotional intelligence in entrepreneurship. Emotional intelligence, or the ability to perceive, understand, and manage emotions, is essential for building strong relationships and effectively leading a team. By developing emotional intelligence, entrepreneurs can create a positive work environment, foster collaboration, and drive their businesses toward success.

2

Chapter 2: The Ethical Foundation of Entrepreneurship

Ethics play a critical role in entrepreneurship, shaping the values and practices that guide business decisions. This chapter examines the ethical principles that underpin successful entrepreneurship, such as integrity, transparency, and social responsibility. By adhering to these principles, entrepreneurs can build trust with stakeholders and create a sustainable business model.

The chapter also explores the concept of ethical leadership and its impact on organizational culture. Ethical leaders set the tone for their organizations, modeling the behavior they expect from their employees. By demonstrating ethical behavior and making principled decisions, entrepreneurs can foster a culture of integrity and accountability within their businesses.

Moreover, the chapter discusses the challenges of navigating ethical dilemmas in entrepreneurship. Entrepreneurs often face situations where they must balance competing interests and make difficult decisions. By developing a strong ethical framework and seeking input from diverse perspectives, entrepreneurs can navigate these dilemmas and make decisions that align with their values.

The chapter also highlights the importance of corporate social responsibility (CSR) in modern entrepreneurship. CSR involves businesses taking responsibility for their impact on society and the environment. By integrating CSR into their business strategies, entrepreneurs can create positive social and environmental outcomes while enhancing their brand reputation and long-term success.

3

Chapter 3: Social Insight and Market Understanding

Understanding the social context in which a business operates is crucial for entrepreneurial success. This chapter delves into the importance of social insight and market understanding in identifying opportunities and developing effective business strategies. By staying attuned to social trends and customer needs, entrepreneurs can create products and services that resonate with their target audience.

The chapter also explores the role of social capital in entrepreneurship. Social capital refers to the networks of relationships and resources that entrepreneurs can draw upon for support and collaboration. By building and leveraging social capital, entrepreneurs can access valuable information, resources, and opportunities that can drive their business growth.

Moreover, the chapter discusses the impact of cultural diversity on entrepreneurship. Embracing cultural diversity can lead to innovative ideas and solutions, as it brings together different perspectives and experiences. By fostering an inclusive and diverse work environment, entrepreneurs can tap into a wealth of creativity and drive their businesses toward success.

The chapter also examines the role of social entrepreneurship, which focuses on creating social value alongside financial returns. Social entrepreneurs identify societal challenges and develop innovative solutions to address them. By integrating social goals into their business models, entrepreneurs can create positive social impact while achieving sustainable growth.

4

Chapter 4: The Role of Innovation in Entrepreneurship

Innovation is the lifeblood of entrepreneurship, driving business growth and competitive advantage. This chapter explores the various dimensions of innovation, including product, process, and business model innovation. By embracing a culture of innovation, entrepreneurs can develop novel solutions that meet customer needs and differentiate their businesses in the market.

The chapter also discusses the importance of fostering a creative work environment. Creativity is the spark that ignites innovation, and entrepreneurs can cultivate creativity by encouraging experimentation, collaboration, and open communication within their teams. By providing the necessary resources and support, entrepreneurs can unlock the creative potential of their employees and drive innovation.

Moreover, the chapter examines the role of technology in driving innovation. Technological advancements have transformed the business landscape, creating new opportunities for entrepreneurs to innovate. By staying abreast of emerging technologies and integrating them into their business strategies, entrepreneurs can gain a competitive edge and drive their businesses toward success.

The chapter also highlights the importance of continuous improvement in innovation. Successful entrepreneurs understand that innovation is an ongoing process that requires constant refinement and iteration. By adopting a mindset of continuous improvement, entrepreneurs can stay ahead of the competition and adapt to changing market conditions.

5

Chapter 5: The Entrepreneurial Ecosystem

The entrepreneurial ecosystem comprises the various elements that support and influence entrepreneurial activity, including government policies, financial institutions, and educational organizations. This chapter delves into the components of a thriving entrepreneurial ecosystem and their impact on business success. By understanding and leveraging the ecosystem, entrepreneurs can access the resources and support they need to grow their businesses.

The chapter also discusses the role of government in fostering entrepreneurship. Governments can create a conducive environment for entrepreneurship by implementing supportive policies, providing funding and resources, and promoting entrepreneurship education. By engaging with government initiatives and advocating for favorable policies, entrepreneurs can enhance their chances of success.

Moreover, the chapter explores the importance of access to finance in entrepreneurship. Financial institutions, such as banks, venture capital firms, and angel investors, play a crucial role in providing the necessary capital for business growth. By understanding the different financing options available and developing strong financial strategies, entrepreneurs can secure the funding they need to scale their businesses.

The chapter also highlights the role of educational organizations in nurturing entrepreneurial talent. Entrepreneurship education programs can equip aspiring entrepreneurs with the knowledge, skills, and mindset needed to succeed in the business world. By participating in these programs and seeking mentorship from experienced entrepreneurs, individuals can enhance their entrepreneurial capabilities and increase their chances of success.

6

Chapter 6: Building a Strong Brand

A strong brand is a valuable asset for any business, helping to differentiate it from competitors and build customer loyalty. This chapter explores the elements of effective branding, including brand identity, positioning, and messaging. By developing a clear and compelling brand, entrepreneurs can create a lasting impression in the minds of their target audience.

The chapter also discusses the importance of consistency in branding. Consistent branding across all touchpoints, such as marketing materials, customer interactions, and product packaging, helps to reinforce the brand's identity and build trust with customers. By maintaining a consistent brand image, entrepreneurs can create a cohesive and memorable brand experience.

Moreover, the chapter examines the role of storytelling in branding. Storytelling is a powerful tool for conveying the brand's values, mission, and unique selling proposition. By crafting authentic and engaging brand stories, entrepreneurs can connect with their audience on an emotional level and build a loyal customer base.

The chapter also highlights the importance of adaptability in branding. As market conditions and customer preferences evolve, businesses must be able to adapt their brand strategies to stay relevant. By continuously monitoring market trends and customer feedback, entrepreneurs can refine their branding efforts and ensure their brand remains strong and competitive.

7

Chapter 7: Customer-Centric Entrepreneurship

Putting the customer at the center of business decisions is essential for entrepreneurial success. This chapter delves into the principles of customer-centric entrepreneurship, including understanding customer needs, delivering exceptional customer experiences, and building long-term relationships. By prioritizing the customer, entrepreneurs can create products and services that truly resonate with their target audience.

The chapter also explores the importance of customer feedback in driving business growth. Gathering and analyzing customer feedback provides valuable insights into customer preferences, pain points, and opportunities for improvement. By actively seeking and acting on customer feedback, entrepreneurs can enhance their products and services and build stronger customer relationships.

Moreover, the chapter discusses the role of personalization in customer-centric entrepreneurship. Personalization involves tailoring products, services, and interactions to meet the individual needs and preferences of customers. By leveraging data and technology, entrepreneurs can deliver personalized experiences that delight customers and foster loyalty.

The chapter also highlights the importance of customer loyalty in business success. Loyal customers are more likely to make repeat purchases, refer others to the business, and provide positive reviews. By implementing strategies to nurture customer loyalty, such as loyalty programs and exceptional customer service, entrepreneurs can create a strong and loyal customer base that drives long-term growth.

8

Chapter 8: Leadership in Entrepreneurship

Effective leadership is crucial for guiding a business toward success. This chapter explores the qualities and skills of successful entrepreneurial leaders, such as vision, communication, and adaptability. By developing strong leadership capabilities, entrepreneurs can inspire and motivate their teams to achieve their business goals.

The chapter also discusses the importance of leading by example. Entrepreneurial leaders set the tone for their organizations by demonstrating the behavior and values they expect from their employees. By modeling integrity, resilience, and a strong work ethic, leaders can create a positive and productive work environment.

Moreover, the chapter examines the role of transformational leadership in entrepreneurship. Transformational leaders inspire and empower their teams by articulating a compelling vision, fostering a culture of innovation, and providing support and encouragement. By adopting a transformational leadership style, entrepreneurs can drive their businesses toward growth and success.

The chapter also highlights the importance of continuous learning and development for entrepreneurial leaders. The business landscape is constantly evolving, and leaders must stay abreast of new trends, technologies, and best practices. By seeking out learning opportunities and embracing a growth mindset, entrepreneurs can enhance their leadership capabilities and ensure their businesses remain competitive.

9

Chapter 9: Strategic Planning and Execution

Strategic planning is a critical component of entrepreneurial success, providing a roadmap for achieving business goals. This chapter continue to explore the key elements of strategic planning, including setting clear goals, conducting a SWOT analysis, and developing action plans. By following a structured approach to strategic planning, entrepreneurs can ensure their businesses are well-positioned for growth and success.

The chapter also discusses the importance of aligning the strategic plan with the company's mission and vision. A clear mission and vision provide direction and purpose, guiding the development of strategic objectives and initiatives. By aligning the strategic plan with the company's mission and vision, entrepreneurs can create a cohesive and focused approach to achieving their goals.

Moreover, the chapter examines the role of execution in strategic planning. A well-crafted plan is only as good as its execution, and entrepreneurs must ensure that they have the necessary resources, capabilities, and processes in place to implement their strategies effectively. By fostering a culture of accountability and continuous improvement, entrepreneurs can drive successful execution and achieve their business objectives.

The chapter also highlights the importance of monitoring and evaluating the progress of the strategic plan. Regularly reviewing and assessing the implementation of the plan allows entrepreneurs to identify any deviations, make necessary adjustments, and ensure they stay on track to achieve their goals. By maintaining a proactive approach to monitoring and evaluation, entrepreneurs can enhance their strategic planning efforts and drive long-term success.

10

Chapter 10: Financial Management and Sustainability

Effective financial management is essential for the sustainability and growth of any business. This chapter explores the key principles of financial management, including budgeting, cash flow management, and financial analysis. By developing strong financial management practices, entrepreneurs can ensure their businesses remain financially healthy and capable of supporting long-term growth.

The chapter also discusses the importance of financial planning in entrepreneurship. Financial planning involves setting financial goals, forecasting future financial performance, and developing strategies to achieve these goals. By engaging in comprehensive financial planning, entrepreneurs can make informed decisions, allocate resources effectively, and mitigate financial risks.

Moreover, the chapter examines the role of financial sustainability in business success. Financial sustainability involves maintaining a balance between generating revenue and managing expenses to ensure the long-term viability of the business. By adopting sustainable financial practices, such as cost control and revenue diversification, entrepreneurs can create a stable financial foundation for their businesses.

The chapter also highlights the importance of financial transparency and accountability. Transparent financial practices build trust with stakeholders, including investors, employees, and customers. By maintaining accurate financial records and providing clear and honest financial reporting, entrepreneurs can enhance their credibility and foster positive relationships with stakeholders.

11

Chapter 11: Marketing and Customer Acquisition

Effective marketing is crucial for attracting and retaining customers in a competitive business environment. This chapter explores the key elements of successful marketing, including market research, branding, and digital marketing. By developing a comprehensive marketing strategy, entrepreneurs can reach their target audience and drive customer acquisition.

The chapter also discusses the importance of understanding the customer journey. The customer journey encompasses the entire experience a customer has with a business, from initial awareness to post-purchase interactions. By mapping out the customer journey and identifying key touchpoints, entrepreneurs can create targeted marketing campaigns that resonate with their audience and drive conversions.

Moreover, the chapter examines the role of digital marketing in modern entrepreneurship. Digital marketing leverages online platforms and technologies to reach and engage customers. By utilizing digital marketing techniques, such as social media marketing, search engine optimization, and email marketing, entrepreneurs can expand their reach and attract a larger customer base.

The chapter also highlights the importance of measuring and analyzing marketing performance. By tracking key performance indicators (KPIs) and analyzing marketing data, entrepreneurs can assess the effectiveness of their marketing efforts and make data-driven decisions. By continuously monitoring and optimizing their marketing strategies, entrepreneurs can enhance their customer acquisition efforts and drive business growth.

12

Chapter 12: Operations and Supply Chain Management

Efficient operations and supply chain management are critical for delivering products and services to customers in a timely and cost-effective manner. This chapter explores the key principles of operations management, including process optimization, inventory management, and quality control. By streamlining their operations, entrepreneurs can improve efficiency, reduce costs, and enhance customer satisfaction.

The chapter also discusses the importance of supply chain management in entrepreneurship. Supply chain management involves coordinating the flow of goods and services from suppliers to customers. By developing strong relationships with suppliers and implementing effective supply chain strategies, entrepreneurs can ensure a reliable and efficient supply of products and services.

Moreover, the chapter examines the role of technology in operations and supply chain management. Technological advancements, such as automation and data analytics, have transformed the way businesses manage their operations and supply chains. By leveraging technology, entrepreneurs can enhance their operational efficiency, improve decision-making, and gain a competitive edge.

CHAPTER 12: OPERATIONS AND SUPPLY CHAIN MANAGEMENT

The chapter also highlights the importance of sustainability in operations and supply chain management. Sustainable practices, such as reducing waste and minimizing environmental impact, are increasingly important for businesses. By adopting sustainable operations and supply chain practices, entrepreneurs can create positive social and environmental outcomes while enhancing their brand reputation and long-term success.

13

Chapter 13: Risk Management and Crisis Response

Risk management is a critical component of entrepreneurial success, helping businesses anticipate, mitigate, and respond to potential challenges. This chapter explores the key principles of risk management, including risk identification, assessment, and mitigation. By developing a comprehensive risk management plan, entrepreneurs can protect their businesses from potential threats and ensure resilience.

The chapter also discusses the importance of crisis response in entrepreneurship. Crises, such as natural disasters, economic downturns, and reputational issues, can have a significant impact on businesses. By developing a robust crisis response plan, entrepreneurs can effectively manage crises and minimize their impact on the business.

Moreover, the chapter examines the role of communication in risk management and crisis response. Clear and timely communication is essential for managing risks and responding to crises. By developing a communication strategy and establishing communication channels, entrepreneurs can ensure that relevant stakeholders are informed and engaged during times of uncertainty.

The chapter also highlights the importance of learning from past experiences in risk management and crisis response. By conducting post-crisis reviews and analyzing the effectiveness of their risk management strategies, entrepreneurs can identify areas for improvement and enhance their preparedness for future challenges.

14

Chapter 14: Scaling and Growth Strategies

Scaling a business involves expanding its operations and increasing its capacity to serve a larger customer base. This chapter explores the key strategies for scaling a business, including market expansion, product diversification, and strategic partnerships. By developing a comprehensive growth strategy, entrepreneurs can achieve sustainable business expansion.

The chapter also discusses the importance of organizational scalability. As businesses grow, they must ensure that their organizational structures and processes can support increased demand. By implementing scalable systems and processes, entrepreneurs can maintain efficiency and quality as their businesses expand.

Moreover, the chapter examines the role of funding in business growth. Access to capital is often essential for scaling a business, and entrepreneurs must explore various funding options, such as venture capital, loans, and crowdfunding. By developing a strong funding strategy and building relationships with investors, entrepreneurs can secure the necessary resources for growth.

The chapter also highlights the importance of maintaining a growth mindset in entrepreneurship. A growth mindset involves embracing challenges, learning from setbacks, and continuously seeking opportunities for improvement. By fostering a growth mindset, entrepreneurs can drive innovation, adapt to changing market conditions, and achieve long-term success.

15

Chapter 15: International Entrepreneurship

Expanding a business into international markets presents both opportunities and challenges. This chapter explores the key considerations for international entrepreneurship, including market research, cultural adaptation, and regulatory compliance. By understanding the complexities of international markets, entrepreneurs can develop effective strategies for global expansion.

The chapter also discusses the importance of building a global network. Establishing relationships with international partners, suppliers, and customers can provide valuable insights and resources for navigating foreign markets. By leveraging their global networks, entrepreneurs can access new opportunities and enhance their chances of success.

Moreover, the chapter examines the role of cultural sensitivity in international entrepreneurship. Understanding and respecting cultural differences is essential for building strong relationships and successfully operating in foreign markets. By developing cultural awareness and adapting their business practices, entrepreneurs can create positive experiences for their international customers and partners.

The chapter also highlights the importance of managing international logistics and supply chains. International expansion often involves complex logistics and supply chain challenges, such as shipping, customs, and distribution. By developing efficient and reliable logistics and supply chain strategies, entrepreneurs can ensure the smooth delivery of products and services to their international customers.

16

Chapter 16: Technology and Digital Transformation

Technology plays a pivotal role in modern entrepreneurship, driving innovation and enabling businesses to operate more efficiently. This chapter explores the impact of technology on entrepreneurship, including the adoption of digital tools, automation, and data analytics. By embracing digital transformation, entrepreneurs can enhance their business processes and gain a competitive advantage.

The chapter also discusses the importance of cybersecurity in the digital age. As businesses become more reliant on technology, they must protect their digital assets from cyber threats. By implementing robust cybersecurity measures, entrepreneurs can safeguard their data, systems, and customer information.

Moreover, the chapter examines the role of digital marketing and e-commerce in modern entrepreneurship. Digital marketing and e-commerce platforms provide businesses with new opportunities to reach and engage customers. By developing comprehensive digital marketing strategies and leveraging e-commerce technologies, entrepreneurs can expand their customer base and drive sales.

The chapter also highlights the importance of continuous technological innovation. The rapid pace of technological advancement requires businesses to stay abreast of new developments and continuously innovate. By fostering a culture of innovation and investing in technology, entrepreneurs can ensure their businesses remain competitive in the digital age.

17

Chapter 17: The Future of Entrepreneurship

The future of entrepreneurship is shaped by emerging trends and evolving market dynamics. This chapter explores the key trends that are likely to influence the entrepreneurial landscape, including sustainability, social impact, and technological advancements. By understanding these trends, entrepreneurs can position themselves for future success.

The chapter also discusses the importance of adaptability in the face of change. The business environment is constantly evolving, and entrepreneurs must be able to adapt to new challenges and opportunities. By cultivating a flexible and adaptive mindset, entrepreneurs can navigate uncertainty and thrive in a dynamic market.

Moreover, the chapter examines the role of collaboration and partnerships in the future of entrepreneurship. Collaborative efforts, such as strategic alliances and industry partnerships, can provide valuable resources and support for collaborating with other businesses and organizations. By building strong partnerships, entrepreneurs can access new resources, share knowledge, and drive innovation.

The chapter also highlights the importance of future-oriented thinking in entrepreneurship. Successful entrepreneurs anticipate future trends and develop strategies to capitalize on emerging opportunities. By staying forward-thinking and proactive, entrepreneurs can position their businesses for long-term success in an ever-changing market.

18

Chapter 18: Continuous Improvement and Innovation

Continuous improvement and innovation are essential for staying competitive in a dynamic market. This chapter explores the principles of continuous improvement, including the Plan-Do-Check-Act (PDCA) cycle and Lean methodologies. By fostering a culture of continuous improvement, entrepreneurs can enhance their business processes, reduce waste, and improve overall efficiency.

The chapter also discusses the importance of fostering a culture of innovation. Encouraging creativity and experimentation within the organization can lead to breakthrough ideas and solutions. By providing the necessary resources and support for innovation, entrepreneurs can drive business growth and stay ahead of the competition.

Moreover, the chapter examines the role of employee engagement in continuous improvement and innovation. Engaged employees are more likely to contribute ideas and take ownership of their work. By creating an environment that values employee input and rewards innovation, entrepreneurs can harness the collective creativity and expertise of their teams.

The chapter also highlights the importance of measuring and evaluating the impact of continuous improvement and innovation efforts. By tracking key performance indicators (KPIs) and analyzing the outcomes of improvement initiatives, entrepreneurs can assess their effectiveness and make data-driven decisions. By continuously monitoring and refining their improvement and innovation strategies, entrepreneurs can achieve sustainable growth and success.

19

Chapter 19: Building a Resilient Organization

Resilience is a critical attribute for navigating the uncertainties and challenges of entrepreneurship. This chapter explores the key elements of organizational resilience, including adaptability, resourcefulness, and agility. By building a resilient organization, entrepreneurs can better withstand disruptions and thrive in a dynamic business environment.

The chapter also discusses the importance of developing a resilient mindset. Entrepreneurs must cultivate a positive and proactive attitude, embracing challenges as opportunities for growth. By fostering resilience at both the individual and organizational levels, entrepreneurs can create a culture that supports long-term success.

Moreover, the chapter examines the role of strategic planning in building resilience. Developing contingency plans and preparing for potential risks can help businesses respond effectively to unforeseen events. By incorporating resilience into their strategic planning efforts, entrepreneurs can enhance their preparedness and ensure business continuity.

The chapter also highlights the importance of fostering strong relationships and networks. Building a supportive network of stakeholders, including customers, suppliers, and industry partners, can provide valuable resources

CHAPTER 19: BUILDING A RESILIENT ORGANIZATION

and support during times of crisis. By nurturing these relationships, entrepreneurs can create a robust foundation for resilience.

20

Chapter 20: The Future of Work and Entrepreneurship

The future of work is undergoing significant transformation, driven by technological advancements and changing societal expectations. This chapter explores the key trends shaping the future of work, including remote work, the gig economy, and automation. By understanding these trends, entrepreneurs can adapt their business models and strategies to stay competitive in the evolving landscape.

The chapter also discusses the importance of fostering a flexible and inclusive work environment. Embracing remote work and flexible work arrangements can attract top talent and enhance employee satisfaction. By promoting diversity and inclusion, entrepreneurs can create a dynamic and innovative workforce.

Moreover, the chapter examines the role of lifelong learning in the future of work. The rapid pace of technological change requires continuous skill development and learning. By investing in employee training and development, entrepreneurs can ensure their teams remain competitive and capable of navigating future challenges.

The chapter also highlights the importance of aligning business practices with societal values. As consumers and employees increasingly prioritize sustainability and social responsibility, businesses must adapt to meet these expectations. By integrating ethical and sustainable practices into their operations, entrepreneurs can build trust and loyalty with stakeholders and position their businesses for long-term success.

"The Cultural Compass: Navigating Entrepreneurship Through Psychology, Ethics, and Social Insight" offers readers a comprehensive guide to mastering the art of entrepreneurship. By integrating psychological, ethical, and social perspectives, this book provides valuable insights and practical strategies for building resilient, innovative, and socially responsible businesses. Whether you're an aspiring entrepreneur or an experienced business leader, "The Cultural Compass" is an essential resource for navigating the complexities of modern entrepreneurship.

Book Description: "The Cultural Compass: Navigating Entrepreneurship Through Psychology, Ethics, and Social Insight"

In "The Cultural Compass: Navigating Entrepreneurship Through Psychology, Ethics, and Social Insight," readers embark on a comprehensive journey into the multifaceted world of entrepreneurship. This insightful book delves into the psychological traits that define successful entrepreneurs, the ethical principles that guide business decisions, and the social insights that drive market understanding. Each chapter offers a deep exploration of critical topics, such as innovation, financial management, marketing, and leadership, providing readers with the knowledge and tools they need to navigate the complex landscape of modern entrepreneurship.

Through a blend of theoretical insights and practical advice, "The Cultural Compass" equips aspiring and seasoned entrepreneurs alike with the skills to build resilient businesses, foster strong relationships, and create positive social impact. The book emphasizes the importance of adaptability, continuous learning, and ethical leadership in achieving long-term success. By integrating psychological, ethical, and social perspectives, "The Cultural Compass" offers a holistic approach to entrepreneurship that is both enlightening and actionable.

www.ingramcontent.com/pod-product-compliance
Lightning Source LLC
LaVergne TN
LVHW020456080526
838202LV00057B/5982